MXJC

Presented to
Tulsa City-County Library
by the
Anne V. Zarrow Library Books for **Children Fund**

Tulsa Community Foundation

Vets

Teaching Tips

Yellow Level 3

This book focuses on the phonemes /v/w/ch/.

Before Reading
- Discuss the title. Ask readers what they think the book will be about.
- Sound out the words on page 3 together.

Read the Book
- Ask readers to use a finger to follow along with each word as it is read.
- Encourage readers to break down unfamiliar words into units of sound. Then, ask them to string the sounds together to create the words.
- Urge readers to point out when the focused phonics phonemes appear in the text.

After Reading
- Encourage children to reread the book independently or with a friend.
- Guide readers through the phonics exercises at the end of the book.

© 2024 Booklife Publishing
This edition is published by arrangement with Booklife Publishing.

North American adaptations © 2024 Jump!
5357 Penn Avenue South
Minneapolis, MN 55419
www.jumplibrary.com

Decodables by Jump! are published by Jump! Library.
All rights reserved. No part of this book may be reproduced in any form without written permission from the publisher.

Library of Congress Cataloging-in-Publication Data is available at www.loc.gov or upon request from the publisher.

ISBN: 979-8-88524-730-6 (hardcover)
ISBN: 979-8-88524-731-3 (paperback)
ISBN: 979-8-88524-732-0 (ebook)

Photo Credits
Images are courtesy of Shutterstock.com. With thanks to Getty Images, Thinkstock Photo and iStockphoto. Cover - leungchopan, evgengerasimovich, p4–5 –4 PM production, p6–7 – ALIAKSANDR PALCHEUSKI, 4 PM production, p8–9 – 4 PM production, OLypa, p10–11 – OLypa, Oksana Kuzmina, p15 – Shutterstock.

Can you find these words in the book?

check

vet

will

It is Val. Val is a vet.

It is Will. Will is a vet.

It will get a check.

Chip is a cat. The vet will check him.

Will can check if Chaz the dog is ill.

A vet will check all parts of a pet.

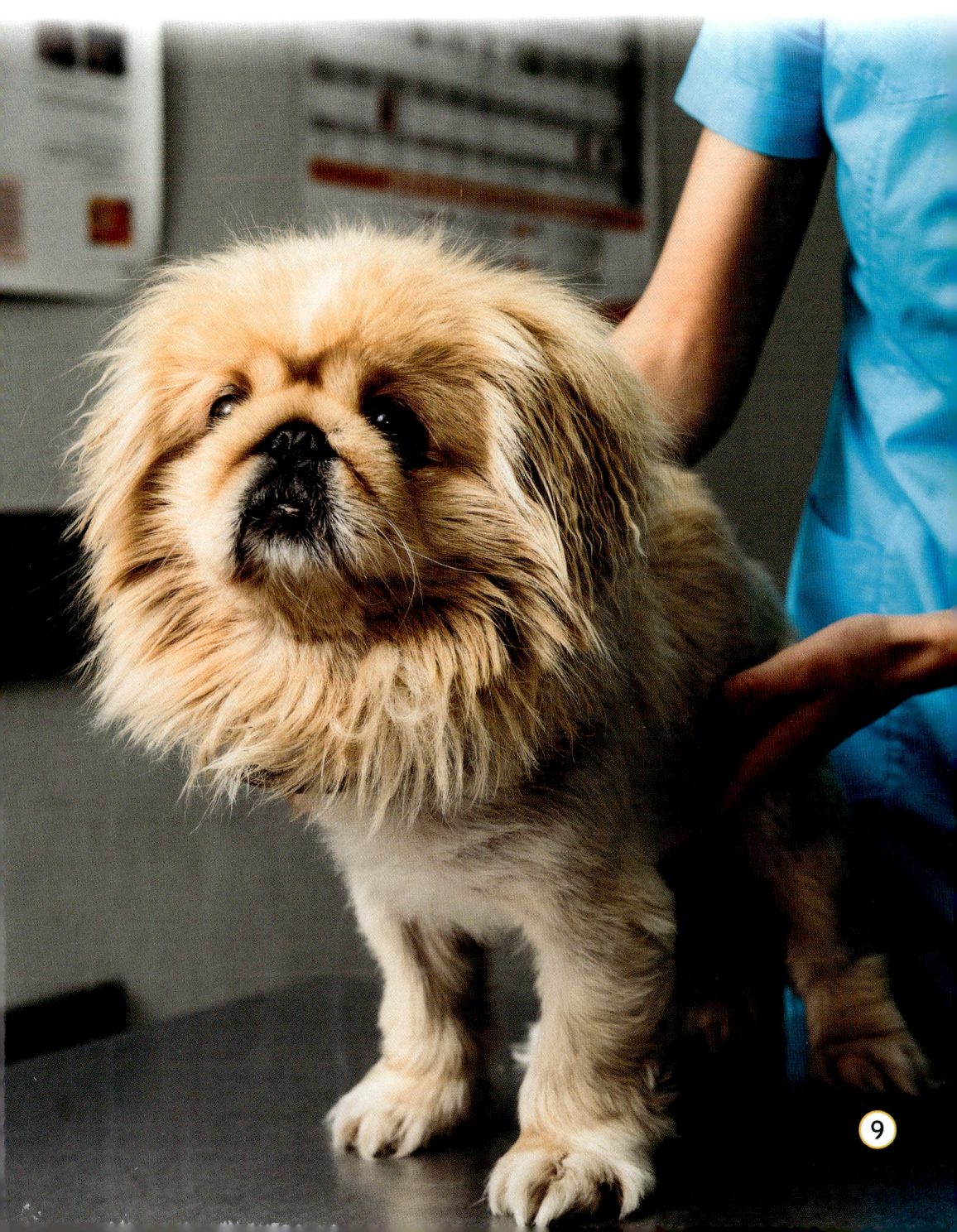

The vet will check the leg of the dog.

I can be a vet as well.

Can you say these sounds and draw them with your finger?

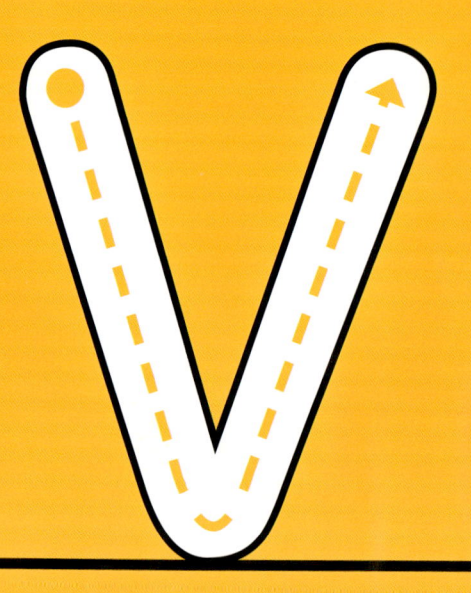

Trace the missing letters to finish these words:

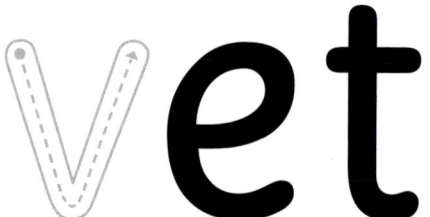

vet

will

check

What other words do you know with the sounds /v/, /w/, or /ch/?

van

water

a e i o u

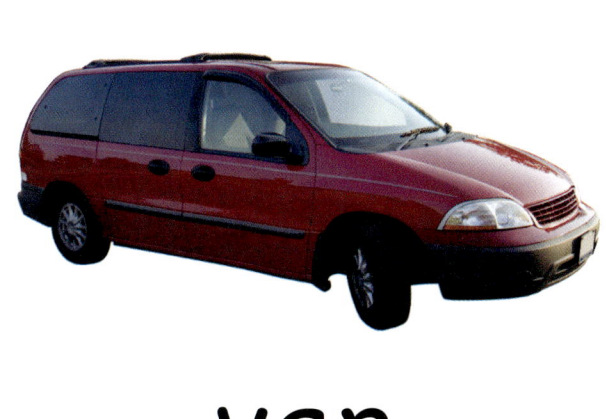

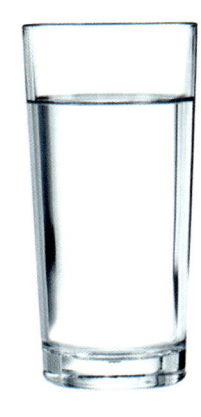

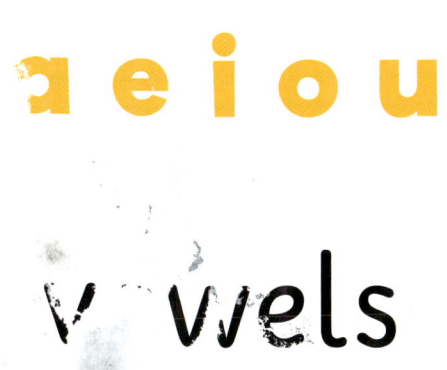

vowels

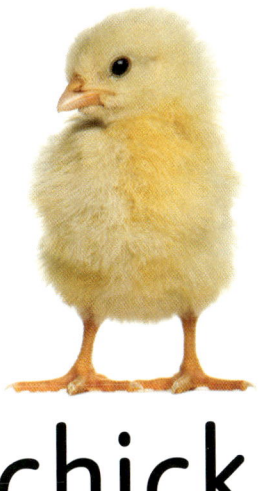

chick

Practice reading the book again:

It is Val. Val is a vet.

It is Will. Will is a vet.

It will get a check.

Chip is a cat. The vet will check him.

Will can check if Chaz the dog is ill.

A vet will check all parts of a pet.

The vet will check the leg of the dog.

I can be a vet as well.